An Adventure in Writing

by Martin & Delia Wach
Illustrated by
Delia Bowman Wach

School Programs

To arrange for the Wachs to come to your school call 800-570-5951.

They have programs for:
K-12, Parents
Parent/Children
Teachers
Artist In Residence
Writing Workshops

For more information on their School Show Programs visit www.headlinekids.com

For Calista, Logan, and Teya, future authors and illustrators.

An Adventure in Writing

by
Martin and Delia Wach

To order additional copies of this book or for book publishing information, or to contact the author:

Headline Books, Inc., P.O. Box 52, Terra Alta, WV 26764 www.headlinekids.com

Tel/Fax: 800-570-5951 Email: mwach@headlinebooks.com

Headline Kids is an imprint of Headline Books

ISBN 0929915542

Library of Congress Control Number: 2006939352

PRINTED IN THE UNITED STATES OF AMERICA

Introduction

   Almost everyone would like to go on an adventure. One of the greatest adventures is mountain climbing. Months of intensive preparation will be required: planning, training, and most of all, the flexibility to persevere until the goal is reached. Finally, the adventurer is able to look over the top of the mountain at all that has been accomplished.

   Writing a children's picture book requires the same kind of preparation and perseverance. Very few individuals complete this adventure.

   We will assist you in starting the adventure of writing and explain the steps needed to successfully complete the task...your job is to persevere

   Books come from the experiences and interests of their authors. *A Very Small Ant Adventure* was inspired by a gift from India. The gift was a small carved wooden pull toy ant that was both intriguing and unique. This toy brought back memories of the leaf cutter ants we had seen in the Rain Forest of Suriname, South America.

   We decided to put together the idea of this cute little wooden ant and our memories of watching the leaf cutter ants at work in the Rain Forest. We chose our character Juba to tell the story. Juba's character traits of curiosity, exploration and scholarship made her the perfect choice to tell the story in this small ant adventure. She will tell the reader what the ants do with all those leaves they are carrying.

   There is a second part to this adventure. After you finish *A Very Small Ant Adventure* we will take you on an even more exciting adventure. Using simple available materials we will lead you through the adventure of creating your very own children's book. We will take you from the story idea through the eight steps we use to create our own books. You must always remember to enjoy the process and think about your potential readers.

   We hope you enjoy our book!

Martin & Delia Wach

Journal

Crayons

Ideas

A gift from India

The Sloth bear from India. Very shaggy (eats ants an ant gourmet)

leaf cutter ant

Juba loves to read

Scientific Method
Observation
Question
experiment (research)
results.
Conclusion
(Does the conclusion answer question)

Build into story

Adventures are every where

Hibiscus tea

Juba's ant Adventure

Juba is learning to make tea and share with her little Teddy Safa.

leaves with bites

Main Characters

Setting

Who?
What?
Where?
When?
Why?

Keep Notes

Draw Pictures

A Very Small Ant Adventure

By Martin & Delia Wach

Juba spends the morning having hibiscus tea with her
Teddy Bear friend, Sara.

When a unique gift arrives from around the World, A small bear begins an ant adventure of play, observation, and learning.

India's Sloth Bear

Raman is an Indian Sloth Teddy Bear.

Raman greets a friend and tells him about a gift he is sending to his cousin, Heynes, the Medicine Bear. Heynes lives in the Rain Forest in South America. It is a special gift for his little student Juba. What could he be sending in the package?

A week later Heynes received the package. To his surprise and delight, it was a beautiful rolling toy ant. He brought this special gift to Juba and said, "This little ant came all the way from India, sent by my cousin Raman, just for you. Let's see what new adventures you and your new toy can discover."

Juba and her little bear, Sara, spent the afternoon studying and appreciating the workmanship of their new toy.

First, they decided to take the little ant for a long walk. They were delighted it wiggled and bounced behind them just like a real ant. Oh, what fun!

While on this walk with her new toy, Juba spied a line of ants carrying pieces of leaves. Although she had seen these creatures hundreds of times before, her new interest in her toy made her very curious. Juba and Sara lay down and studied them very closely. Why were they carrying pieces of leaves?

She went to her Aunt Fiba to ask her all kinds of questions about these wonderful and interesting ants. Aunt Fiba gave her a book to read. I wonder if it will answer her questions? She certainly studied very hard and to her delight she learned all about leaf cutting ants.

Juba wrote a letter to Raman, thanking him for the wonderful toy and telling him how it made her much more curious about the ants that live in her Rain Forest home.

Bear Village
Suriname, S.A.

Dear Uncle Raman,

Thank-you very much for the toy ant. I love to play with her and share her with my Teddy Bear Sara.

As I was playing I began to wonder about the ants that march thru our village, each carrying a piece of leaf. Where do they take the leaves and why?

First I spent some time watching them at work. Then I borrowed a book from Aunt Fiba about ants. This is what I learned.

The hard working ants are called leaf cutter ants. First they cut pieces of leaves with their mouth parts called mandibles.

mandibles

Then they carry the pieces back to their nest underground in special rooms. Smaller ants then clean and prepare the leaves for growing. Then one ant brings a piece of fungus. The fungus starts to grow and the ants tend it. The Queen arrives and in her chamber she lays eggs. The new born ants eat the fungus.

The hard working little ants are gardeners.

Having fun and learning,

Juba

Antenna
piece of leaf
Head
thorax
mandible
Abdomen

Delia's journal entry on her birthday.

Preparing to Write a Children's Picture Book

Writing

If you like to write, keep a journal to write in every day. Good, bad, funny, sad, and interesting things happen to everyone. Writing them down makes creating books possible. Start by writing down the date, then enter ideas that interest you—like things that make you laugh, scare you, and anything else you can think about your day's adventure. An excellent way to get started is to read books by other authors. We read books every day in order to understand how other successful authors put their ideas together. There are hundreds of children's picture books in the library. Try to read as many as possible. Book authors read all the time. Also keep notes about what you like and where it can be found if needed again.

Juba writing and drawing in her sketch book on the same day as Delia's birthday.

If you want to be an illustrator...

Drawing

If you like to draw, keep a sketch book and add sketches every day of the world around you. Draw anything and everything that interests you. An interesting exercise is to draw chairs either in your home or at school. If you get skilled enough to draw chairs you can draw anything.

Try to add some sketches to your writing journal and descriptive writing to your sketch book pictures. You must stay consistent and add to your journals every day. There is no replacement for practice. The more you write or draw the more skilled you will become.

Please excuse the Teddy Bear. Teddy Bears are always sneaking into Delia's sketches.

Eight steps to develop a children's picture book.

1. Brain Storming
2. Outlining
3. Story Board
4. Writing

5. Illustrating
6. Dummy Book
7. Editing
8. Completed Book

A very shiney spot

Soft yellow like fur

dark sides

Light spot

Two sets of light feathers

Anytime you have a chance to draw a dead insect, do so. You may need the drawing as reference material.

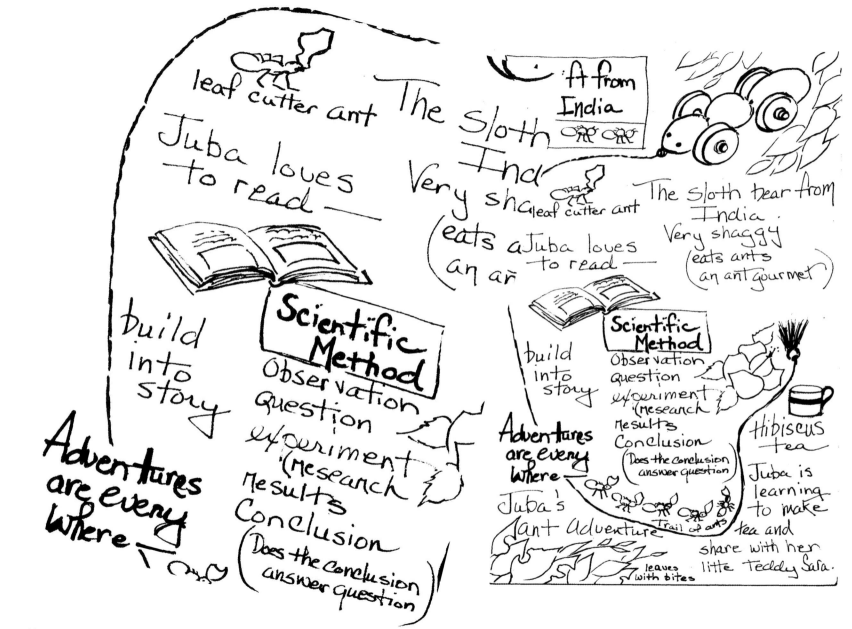

leaf cutter ant

Juba loves
to read —

The Sloth
Ind

A from
India

Very sha leaf cutter ant

(eats a Juba loves
an ar to read —

The sloth bear from
India.
Very shaggy
(eats ants
(an ant gourmet)

build
into
story

Scientific
Method
Observation
Question
experiment
(research
results
Conclusion
(Does the conclusion
answer question

build
into
story

Scientific
Method
Observation
Question
experiment
(research
results
Conclusion
(Does the conclusion
answer question

Hibiscus
tea

Juba is
learning
to make
tea and
share with her
little Teddy Sara.

Adventures
are every
where

Adventures
are every
where —

Juba's
Ant Adventure

Trail of ants

leaves
with bites

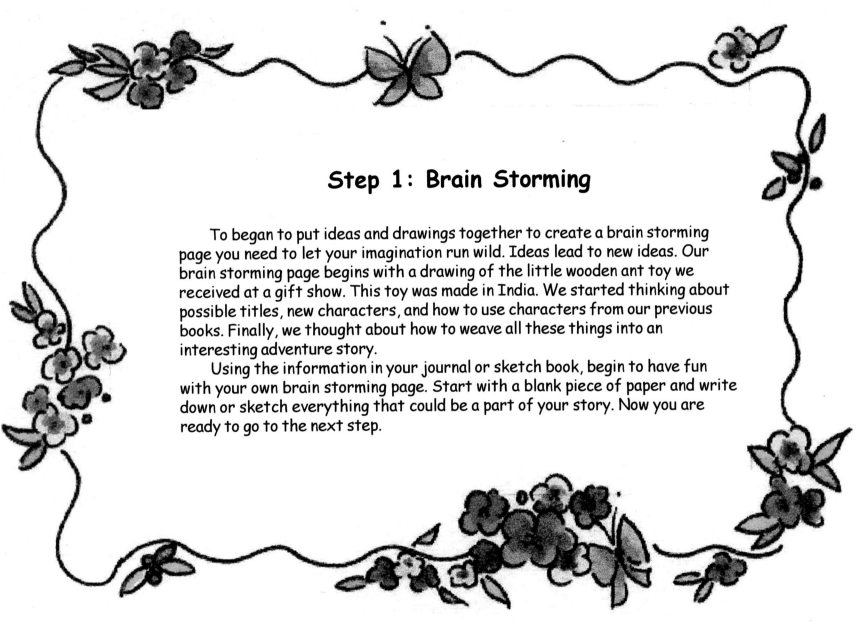

Step 1: Brain Storming

To began to put ideas and drawings together to create a brain storming page you need to let your imagination run wild. Ideas lead to new ideas. Our brain storming page begins with a drawing of the little wooden ant toy we received at a gift show. This toy was made in India. We started thinking about possible titles, new characters, and how to use characters from our previous books. Finally, we thought about how to weave all these things into an interesting adventure story.

Using the information in your journal or sketch book, begin to have fun with your own brain storming page. Start with a blank piece of paper and write down or sketch everything that could be a part of your story. Now you are ready to go to the next step.

Step 2: Outlining for a Book

One of the most important skills for a future author is the skill of outlining. The short story of *A Very Small Ant Adventure,* progresses from the gift of a small wooden ant toy to Juba's curiosity for the leaf cutter ants around her village and finally to the thank you note to Raman explaining what she had learned.

We have always been interested in and appreciated science projects. Scientific investigation starts with a question, proposes a possible answer (hypothesis), requires experimentation, and evaluates the results of the experiments to reach a conclusion.

In our outline for *A Very Small Ant Adventure,* we began with a gift sent from Juba's uncle in India. This wooden toy had to be played with, then studied very carefully. Juba then observed similarities between her new toy and the strange leaf cutter ants that were all around her in the rain forest. She started reading about these unique ants and took notes. Finally, she wrote a letter to Raman telling him all about what she had learned. While this did not follow the scientific method perfectly, Juba did set up a really good process for study and learning.

Here is the outline we used for *A Very Small Ant Adventure.*

I. Introducing a new character: Raman
    A. Where from
    B. Gift being sent from India

II. Gift arrives
    A. Heynes gives the toy to Juba
    B. Challenges her to learn more

III. Run and play time
    A. Walk with the toy
    B. Study and appreciate toy

IV. Observing and remembering leaf cutter ants
    A. Seeing leaf cutter ants in a new way
    B. The question: Why do they carry all those leaves?

V. Studies a book about these interesting creatures

VI. Conclusion
    A. Facts about leaf cutter ants as gardeners woven into a thank you note to Raman.
    B. Juba used an outline to create her thank you letter.

Step 3: The Story Board

The story board is the physical layout of the proposed pages that will be in the book. Each page will have a preliminary sketch, preliminary writing, or both. This is the expansion of the outline.

A Very Small Ant Adventure has only 14 pages and probably should be called a booklet. The typical children's picture book has 32 pages. 32 pages is the standard in the publishing industry.

The story board gives the author the first chance to really see the whole book and to begin trying to read the whole book out loud. How does it sound? Does it make sense and flow easily? Is it good? This also gives the author a chance to see new possibilities and put in new ideas. The author can now check sketches and decide whether to change, add or remove sketches. This picture of your book is vital to its composition.

You must remember to keep all notebooks, preliminary sketches, and reference materials in a special file. Sometimes a scrap that seemed to have no importance to your book can become very important.

Story Board for A Very Small Ant Adventure

Step 4: Writing

As authors we like to take the voice of a story teller. We love telling stories to a live audience. As a result, we chose to take the voice of a story teller relating the tale of our imaginary group of Teddy Bears. Another possibility would have been to have one of the characters relate the tale.

When writing your story you must consider whose voice is speaking. Be sure to stay consistent and if you change from one voice to another you have to explain it to the reader or they will be confused.

You must also decide "who" each of the characters are. This is an opportunity to take time to write a biography of each character: Who are they? What do they look like? What are their interests? Add all the information you can. This exercise will help your characters come alive when you write about them.

What is happening? We relate what happened after Juba got her special gift. You must decide on the action taking place in your story.

Where does the action take place in your story? We start the action in India and continue the action in South America. Where will your story take place?

How do the events of your story proceed? After Juba plays, develops a curiosity, and studies about leaf cutter ants she is able to conclude the story by thanking Raman for his wonderful gift. She writes a letter to him showing how much she has learned. How all this happens is the action of a story and leads to the conclusion. What is the action in your story and how will it end?

Don't forget the:

Who
What
Why
When
Where
How

Step 5: Illustrating Using Reference Materials

Materials Needed:
1. Tracing paper
2. Graphite paper [instructions on next page]
3. Drawing paper (card stock is good)
4. Ebony pencil
5. No. 2 pencil
6. Colored pencils
7. Crayons
8. White plastic eraser
9. Safe release masking tape
10. Cotton balls
11. Finger nail polish remover

This photo of an arrangement of subjects, or still life, is what the illustrator started with to create the drawing on page 27.

Note: (Tracing paper is a thin translucent paper used by artists and illustrators to trace images so they can transfer them to other surfaces. Graphite paper is tracing paper with one side liquefied ebony pencil that is used to transfer traced images to the drawing paper).

Seldom is a writer of children's picture books skilled at both writing and illustrating. If you love to draw, this section will help give your illustrations a professional polish. If your skill is writing, and drawing is difficult for you, the techniques listed will help you create simple illustrations to make your story come alive.

This will be one of the most important exercises because having some illustrations adds a great deal to the interest of your book. Illustrations of real animals and characters will help capture the imagination of the readers.

These are some of the places illustrators go to find references:
1. Internet images
2 Advertisements
3. Pictures from magazines, newspapers and books
4. Your own photos

Procedure:

Included are four images from several sources to demonstrate the method for creating Children's Picture Book Illustrations. The bunny image came from the internet, the daffodils from a seed catalogue, the grape hyacinths from a gardening book, and the turtle from a book about baby animals. The illustrator put them together to create a totally new image. [All of these images are on the next page.]

1. Making graphite paper: The first step is to make a piece of tracing paper into graphite paper by covering one side totally with ebony pencil. Then go over the ebony covered side with a cotton ball soaked in fingernail polish remover. The graphite now becomes a tool to transfer images to the drawing paper. (The soaked cotton ball procedure can be done several times to keep the graphite side fresh.)

2. Now trace the images you wish to transfer to the drawing paper.

3. After tracing the four images chosen for the illustration the illustrator first placed the traced daffodil image on the drawing paper. This would be the background of the finished drawing.

4. When she put the traced image on the drawing paper the illustrator bent down the two top corners of the tracing paper and placed two small register marks on two sides so that she could match up the paper again if need be. (see the illustration top of page 25) Now slide the graphite paper under the tracing paper. The graphite side should be down on the drawing paper. Now press down on the image and it transfers to the drawing paper. The traced image of the daffodils was too small to go all the way across the drawing paper so it had to be moved and retraced more than once to cover the whole background of the drawing paper.

5. Now the illustrator added the next image of the grape hyacinths working from the top down on the drawing paper. This encourages overlapping and keeps the image from becoming smeared.

6. The bunny was then added by simply turning the tracing paper over so that it would face the turtle.

7. Then the Turtle was added.

8. Finally the grape hyacinths were added in the foreground to complete the image.

The background is the distant part of a scene and the foreground is the part of a scene nearest the viewer.

Note: This procedure is available on DVD [www.headlinekids.com].

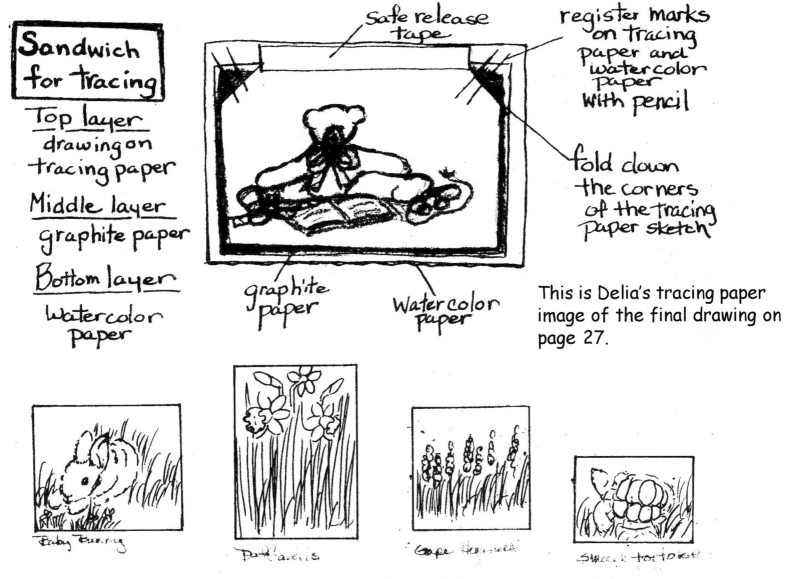

Sandwich for tracing

Top layer
drawing on tracing paper

Middle layer
graphite paper

Bottom layer
watercolor paper

safe release tape

graphite paper

watercolor paper

register marks on tracing paper and watercolor paper with pencil

fold down the corners of the tracing paper sketch

This is Delia's tracing paper image of the final drawing on page 27.

Baby Bunny

Daffodils

Cape Heaths

Spur tortoise

These are the traced images used to create the final drawing on page 26.

Bringing the four pictures together to create an original illustration.

Pen and ink illustration

Notice in the reference material the bunny was facing left. Now in the new illustration the bunny is facing right having an encounter with the turtle. The illustrator just reversed the tracing paper.

Simple pen and ink and watercolor, just using the local colors. Daffodils are just yellow, the foliage and grass are green, the bunny is brown, the turtle is tan, the hyacinths are purple. Creating a more cartoon like image.

Colored pencil illustration rendered with a set of 24 colored pencils with many layers.

Delia's steps for a professional illustration.

1. Simple pencil line drawing

2. Put pen line over pencil drawing, let dry and erase pencil lines.

3. Water color warm colors in thin washes of Naples Yellow, Burnt Sienna, and Red. The illustrator used gouache.

4. Add cool colors blues and greens and redraw any lost pen lines.

Step 6: The Dummy Book

Working from the story board you have to keep adding, removing, changing and correcting until you are satisfied that it is the book you are prepared to show others. You are now able to copy each page of text and illustrations and put together a Dummy Book. You often can find a scrap book with enough pages or you can make your own. We are including a sample picture for making your own Dummy Book. This Dummy Book will look very much like a scrap book but will have your writing and illustrations pasted in. We presented our first book to our first publisher in this format.

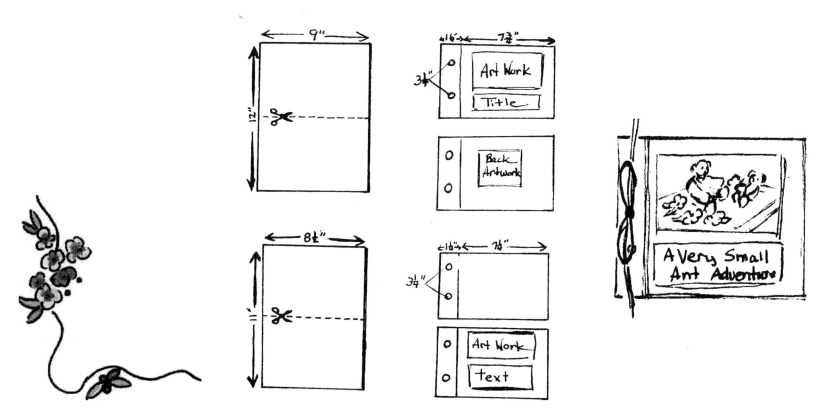

Note: Remember again to keep a file with all scraps of information that went into your book.

Step 7: Editing

Now it is time to let individuals review your dummy book. You can have your classmates read the book or some of your friends. Listen to what they say. Your family will also help you with their opinions. This is the time to make all corrections to spelling, punctuation and story line.

Step 8: The Finished Book

Congratulations! You have written a professionally done Children's Picture Book.

Your Book is Finished!

Writing Techniques

We have just covered the basic requirements for writing a children's book. Now, we will discuss our unique approach to writing. Everyone has a unique way of putting the words to paper. That is why there are so many wonderful books.

Writing 1—Story Telling

When it comes to the creative part of writing, we take two quite different approaches. By putting these two styles together, we have produced four published books! We want you to realize that each and every person with desire to write can really do it. You only have to be sure to tell a good story.

Martin was born with a spectacular sense of exaggeration. He could make a story up as soon as he was asked, so writing these stories down came easy to him. Perhaps this is the key. You almost have to be born wanting to tell great tales and wanting to write them down.

Everyone has great and small adventures. Try to apply your imagination even to the smallest of your adventures. Ask questions, and then supply the answers. Nothing is impossible when you create your own story. Write them in your journal so someday soon you can write your own children's book.

Writing 2—Words From Pictures

Delia begins all her stories with a picture of an ideal scene; a moment in time when everything is perfect. She loves scenes of someone reading a book, having a tea party, or even arriving at a dream home. This is a moment when everything is amazing. She hopes when people look at her illustrations they will have the same feelings.

She started the illustrations for *A Very Small Ant Adventure* with Juba pulling a small rolling duck toy behind her. She has always loved little pull toys and knows a lot of other people do too. Actually, the first picture was Juba pulling a duck toy and she changed it to an ant when someone gave it to her on a trip. She then created a picture of Juba and her pal, Sara, having a tea party on a simple quilt. These pictures grew to tell a story because she looked at them all together and asked questions. How did Juba get this ant toy? She didn't have it at the picnic. If it was gift, where did it come from? If Heynes, the medicine bear, gave it to her, where did he get it? Now, what does she do with it? First, of course, she has to take it for a walk and then play with it. Finally, she remembered the leaf cutter ants. She then studied a book on these creatures and sent a letter to Raman explaining why she is so fascinated with her new toy. Delia is able to create text from images and concludes her story by acknowledging the gift in a thank you note. For Delia, the illustrations come first.

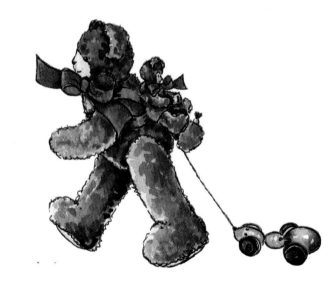

We are two very different authors, but together, we have created a whole new world of children's books.

Story Board of First Draft—What differences can you see in the final book?

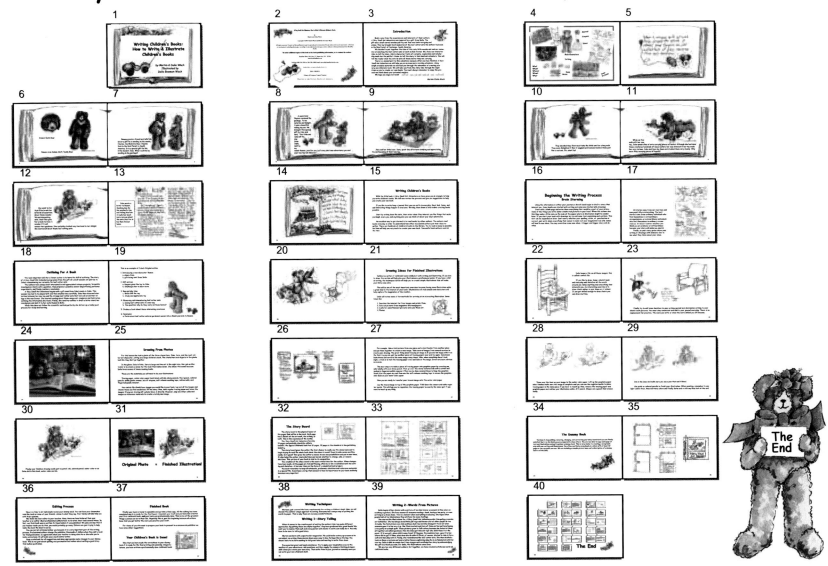